funfacts about

Bearded Dragon

31 Frequently Asked Questions by

Beardie Pet Owners & Lovers

Short Picture Book for Kids

BY FIONA WEBER

The World of rare pets

Introduction

What about keeping an animal that looks straight from the time of the dinosaurs, has a friendly temperament, and enjoys quality time with its owner? Bearded Dragons can be the perfect choice for you! In addition to being an excellent species for beginners in the lizard world, it is relatively easy to maintain and full of personality. And you need a reasonably simple terrarium with little equipment. You can easily find them for sale in many colors and patterns.

Even with all the ease of having one of these dragons, you may still need to find out whether they are a good choice to keep as a pet. We made this exclusive short ebook to solve your doubts, answering all common questions about the amazing Bearded Dragon.

1. Are Bearded Dragons lizards?

Bearded Dragons are lizards. We generally use the term "Bearded Dragon" to refer to several species of the Pogonas genus. The species of these lizards that you can easily find for sale and spread in the hobby is Pogona vitticeps. They are small, very friendly, and trendy pets worldwide. These lizards come from Australia, have terrestrial habits, and inhabit eucalyptus and acacia forests and savanna and desert areas.

Bearded dragons measure around 11 inches in length, including the tail. They exhibit a large triangular head with a flattened and oval-shaped body with short legs and a tail with a thick base that is tapering.

2. Do Bearded Dragons have a third eye?

As strange as it sounds, yes, these animals have a third eye, that's right. If this may seem strange to many, it is common for fish, amphibians, and reptiles like lizards to have a "third eye." The name is in quotes because its function is not precisely that of an ordinary eye. Pay attention to the top of the animal's head. In the middle of it, you will see a pale-colored circle whose lack of pigmentation serves precisely to let the light through. This structure is what reptile scholars call the pineal eye.

This organ disappeared with evolutionary progress (for example, it is not found in today's birds and mammals), but it does have a defined function. Formerly it was considered a vestigial organ with no defined function. Still, today we already know its importance in animal physiology.

The parietal eye is a photoreceptor structure (capable of capturing light). The function is related to the perception of light variation, directly influencing the regulation of the circadian rhythm and, consequently, the physiological activity of the animal.

The circadian rhythm is the 24-hour period on which the biological cycle of almost all living beings, including us humans, is based. For example, see

how our daily activities are based on light variation (day/night) and temperature changes. It's like that with animals too. The presence of a large number of fibers forms a nervous structure that communicates the "eye" directly with the brain (epithalamus), more precisely with the pineal gland.

The pineal gland is related to the production of hormones that modulate the sleep pattern and behaviors related to seasonality, such as reproduction, according to the duration of the light period in the environment.

3. What is the Bearded Dragon's lifespan?
Bearded Dragons generally live around ten years in captivity. The lifespan of your Bearded Dragon depends directly on the quality of life you offer the animal, such as the size and composition of the

terrarium, food, and maintenance.

Your lizard can even live up to 15 years if it has enough space, with enough life quality, heating, and a balanced diet.

4. Are there different types and breeds of Bearded Dragons?

In nature, you can find eight species (currently recognized) of Bearded Dragons. Among them, four are in the hobby. They are available in the form of species or even hybrids. These dragons show an unexpected change in body color concerning the color of the soil in which they live. The different varieties we see today in captivity were created by selecting these animals. In the lizards available in stores and breeders, you can find more than 30 morphs.

Each morph has a different pattern depending on scales, beard and head shape, coloring, tonality, and even the animal's size. In addition, each variety has a name (often complicated and confusing) pre-determined by the breeding community.

To facilitate the classification of those morphs, breeders divided them into three main characters: Scalation, pattern, and color. These characteristics will give value and rarity to the individual in question. Breeding lizards to obtain unique and desired traits requires knowledge of the genetic load (lineage) that both parents carry. On the other hand, breeding some morphs is becoming increasingly profitable in the market.

5. How big can a Bearded Dragon get?

They are considered small lizards, usually reaching around 11 inches in size by adulthood. The average body weight of these animals rarely exceeds 15 ounces.

6. Are they dragons?

The animal is called a dragon because of its primitive appearance and robust body protected by thorns. In addition, it is an ancient species, having its ancestors set foot on the earth approximately 250 million years ago, when they took a different evolutionary path from the dinosaurs.

They are known as bearded for having an expandable pouch with pointed scales in the lower region of the neck. Both sexes have this pouch, but males exhibit it more often, especially in courtship rituals. Females, however, also display an expanding pocket as a sign of aggression and territory dominance.

7. Are Bearded Dragons

good pets?

Yes, for sure, if they weren't, they wouldn't have been such a popular pet since the early '90s. Because they are small lizards with a calm and friendly temperament, it is considered easy to maintain and handle them. In addition, these lizards require little care to have a quality life and good health. That's why they are popular and preferred among beginners.

However, the tank's space must not be too small; it must provide enough room for the lizards to feel safe and to have a heating system.

8. Are Bearded Dragons friendly?

The success of these small reptiles as pets is due not only to their peculiar beauty but mainly to their temperament.

Bearded dragons are generally very docile and balanced, highlighting the high sociability of their temperament.

For all these reasons, it is generally one of the most recommended species for beginner caregivers. Due to their friendly behavior and small size, they are easier to handle and care for than large, complex-tempered reptiles such as iguanas. Another advantage of keeping a bearded dragon as a pet is that the population of this reptile is considered stable in the wild, and all animals available on the market come from captivity.

9. Are Bearded Dragons venomous?

Around 2005, Australian scientists proved what some hobbyists had long claimed, that Bearded Dragons are venomous. These lizards produce a not very strong venom, with a chemical

constitution resembling some rattlesnakes' venom. This venom strongly affects small animals, acting quickly during a lizard's bite. In humans, they only cause swelling in the affected region and can be followed by bleeding. Still, it is nothing to worry about; it is considered harmless.

10. Should I get a male or a female Bearded Dragon?

It's up to you to choose what best suits your style and what you're looking for, but there are some essential differences between female and male Bearded Dragons.

The first difference we can mention is physical: males have a slightly more robust appearance, a thicker tail (especially at the base), a larger size, and a more developed beard than females. From a behavioral point of view, males are more active and friendly. Still, they can be a bit aggressive and intimidating during breeding seasons. Females are more passive and calm and can lay eggs even if they don't have a male in their place. Our tip is to obtain individuals who are not very young, as they demand a more significant workload, especially concerning food and being more fragile to the environment.

11. Where can I find the best quality Bearded Dragons?

Because it is a trendy animal, it is common to find individuals for sale, from specialized to large department stores.

Our golden tip is always to get your animals from breeders you know or have been referred to. That way, you know where the animal came from, its parents, how the breeder takes care of it, and everything else you need to know to get healthy, high-quality animals.

12. Will my Bearded Dragon bond with me?

Yes, these reptiles have a keen awareness of their exterior and will recognize and bond with their owners.

Scientists conducted some research on the comfort level of close people, and the result showed that the stress level was low when the lizards were with their owners.

To establish a relationship with your dragon, you must constantly interact with it, hold it in your hand, show interest when feeding them, talk to it, and even take it for walks. The more time you dedicate to it, the dragon will love it, and you will become best friends. In addition, you will offer your significant pet enrichment, bringing even more quality of life!

13. My Bearded Dragon likes to be held or pet?
Yes, they like to be cuddled. It's an excellent way for the owner to bond with their beardie.
You should maintain physical contact with your pet when your dragon arrives in your home. Putting the lizard on your shoulders or petting them makes the lizard feel safer and, in addition, accelerates the recognition that you are its owner and its friend. Whenever you can, give your Bearded Dragon affection and attention.

14. Do Bearded Dragons have different personalities?
Absolutely, just like any animal.
The main factor in the animal's personality is always genetic. Another reason to acquire it from a responsible breeder is

so that way you can know the temperament of your pet's parents.

Some are calmer, and some learn tricks faster than others, and so on.

15. Can I potty train my Bearded Dragon?

It's not that simple, but yes, you can.

Beardies are animals of habit; they usually feed at the same place and time and defecate at the same place and time. This helps a lot in potty training, similar to training a dog or cat.

Know in advance that you will need to set aside time in your day to teach your lizard, and it may take some time to reach the goal.

Pay attention to your lizard's behavior and the times he is used to urinating; this way, it's easy to predict when you should put him in the right place until he learns to go to the right place on his own.

16. What is the price of a Bearded Dragon?

The price of a Bearded Dragon can vary according to the region, the breeder, and especially the morph you are looking for.

The average cost for a juvenile of a typical pattern is around 50 dollars. However, some morphs can reach values close to 1000$

A significant issue is to trust only responsible breeders. If you find a reptile or other exotic animal for a meager price, be suspicious of its origin. The only way to guarantee the preservation of the species is to avoid animal trafficking and mistreatment and denounce illegal sales.

17. What do I need to keep my Bearded Dragon healthy?

With good planning, bringing the bearded dragon home should be the last thing you do. Therefore, before buying the pet, prepare a suitable environment to receive it with the designed care.

As much as your dragon occasionally gets loose in areas designed for this, the right thing is always to keep it inside a terrarium adapted to its needs.

This terrarium must simulate the conditions of its natural habitat, that is, the arid region of the Australian desert.

Therefore, providing the high temperature and low humidity is necessary, but with good air ventilation. Due to the size of these lizards, the minimum size for a terrarium to be kept is an adult individual of 40 inches x 24 inches. Regarding heat, the average temperature should be kept between 75-85°F, but always remember to offer a cooler area so he can regulate his body temperature. The temperature can also vary from day to night, dropping to 70-75°F overnight. Finally, always keep the humidity below 50%.

These small reptiles are comfortable in earthy or sandy substrates. Therefore, one of the main components of the bearded dragon terrarium is the substrate. This material is applied to the bottom of the terrarium. This element is vital for mimicking the soil that lizards are used to finding in nature.

There are several types of substrate found in exotic pet supply stores. Still, some can be harmful to the Pogona, as they can be ingested without the owner realizing it. So talk to the specialist to buy only the suitable material for your pet.

These lizards like to have dry branches, small logs, and rocks at their disposal—both for hiding and basking.

Rocks or hot plates can be used for heating, and UVB/UVA lamps are usually used for basking. Remember to offer bowls for water and food and temperature and humidity gauges to ensure everything is up to standard.

18. How will my Bearded Dragon react with other animals?

They will remain calm and friendly if they don't feel threatened by other pets like dogs and cats. Pogona are curious animals, so your first reaction will be to want to know what that bunch of fur looking at them is. This means that they will come close, sniff, and may demonstrate behavior like shaking their head or turning darker in color, displaying particular behavior.

If they feel threatened, these behaviors will escalate, with the lizard expanding its body, opening its mouth, and even trying to attack.

When the animal feels threatened or frightened, it inflates its head's scales, which take on black color. This is one of his most remarkable abilities, although it's not a good sign. A bearded dragon comfortable in its home does not need to adopt this defensive mechanism. If any of those involved remain too curious or scared, proceed slowly, introducing each other's presence little by little and very carefully. This tip is precious to cats, who often see lizards as prey.

19. What is the best food for my Bearded dragon?

Bearded dragons are omnivorous animals that generally maintain a varied diet in the wild. The variety of foods consumed in their diet often varies depending on the availability of food in their habitat and the time

of year.

Therefore, it will be vital to provide your bearded dragon with complete and balanced nutrition based on its nutritional needs. Along with fruits and vegetables, you will need to include invertebrates such as insects and snails in their diet. You can find a variety of these foods in stores specializing in reptiles.

The feeding style also varies according to the life stage of the animal. Juveniles need more insects than plant material. So we can talk about offering 80% of insects and 20% of vegetables and fruits. Adults need more vegetables and fruits than insects, amounting to 20% insects and 80% vegetables and fruits.

A balanced diet can contain dark green leafy vegetables (kale, broccoli leaves, arugula, etc.), insects such as crickets, cockroaches, mealworms, fruits such as bananas, kiwis, grapes, strawberries, peaches, pears, apples, melons, etc.

Another essential care will be to take your lizard to the vet regularly. These little lizards are especially vulnerable to ectoparasites, especially mites. Therefore, cleaning your terrarium and the house must be cautious.

20. What foods should I avoid giving my Bearded

dragon?

Avoid mainly citrus fruits (lemons, limes, oranges, pineapple) and high-fat foods (avocado).

Some foods like mushrooms, garlic, onions, and eggplant can be toxic; keep away from them. Also, never offer insects collected in nature or of unknown origin; they may contain harmful elements.

Also, avoid offering food such as pinkies and baby birds, do it only with adults and a few times a year. Foods rich in water and low in nutrients, such as lettuce and cucumbers, can lead to intestinal disorders.

21. Why is my Bearded Dragon not eating?

If your Bearded Dragon is showing a lack of appetite, this condition can indicate several reasons for this.

There are two main factors for this to occur. The first thing to watch

out for is if your dragon is shedding. These animals, like other reptiles, do not usually feed during the shed.

This behavior happens because, in nature, they would be exposed to predators, so they remain holed up during this period.

The second most common cause is the irregular temperature of the environment. For example, suppose the temperature is below 70 degrees F. In that case, your beardie will show symptoms like a lack of appetite, intestinal problems, lethargy, etc. That's why it's so essential for your terrarium to have heaters and thermometers to check if everything is within the parameters necessary for your pet.

If everything is in order, your lizard is not shedding, and being kept at the correct temperature, you should be aware of other behavioral signs and symptoms that can indicate something is wrong.

It can be a disease, an intestinal impaction, or even some kind of nutritional deficiency. You should seek professional help as soon as possible.

22. How to properly feed my Bearded Dragon?

Closely monitoring when and how much your dragon eats is the best way to know if it is growing healthy and at the correct rate and if it has any problems or nutritional deficiencies.

In addition, keeping an eye on your beardie during feeding times is essential to avoid poor or overeating, which leads to various issues such as obesity.

Of course, only some dragons are the same; some are more greedy, others eat less, and, as mentioned earlier, their food needs change depending on the individual's life stages. The period when your dragon is considered a baby is when the animal is at its most fragile. At this stage, your animal must receive a wide range of nutrients within the correct frequency.

When we talk about baby dragons, we refer to animals up to a maximum of 5 months old.

During this phase, in addition to the quality of the food, we still have other vital points, such as the frequency you should offer and the size of the food. For example, you should not give baby dragons food, especially insects larger than their head; this can lead to choking and digestive problems.

Because babies have a faster metabolism and more important nutritional requirements (as they are in a period of forming organs and bones), they need to receive a high percentage of animal proteins in their diet. The diet of your baby dragon needs to be composed of between 60% and 80% animal protein and 20% to 40% plant matter, while an adult requires a diet of 20% to 25% animal protein and 75% to 80% vegetables.

Regarding frequency, we have that you should feed these young dragons more often than adult dragons. Offer a small portion of insects 3 to 4 times a day and vegetable material thrice a week.

Remember that the insects must be small and the plant material (such as fruits and vegetables) chopped into small sizes or even grated.

Dragons are considered young, from 5 months until they reach sexual maturity. During this phase, the diet should be

transitioned little by little, always keeping an eye on your animal's behavior, thus avoiding obese and malnourished animals.

In adults (some authors say that this phase takes place around 18 months of animal life), food is no longer something so worrying for its tutor. So feed him about three times a week. Pregnant females are an exception and should be fed more often and given supplements.

23. Should I supplement my Bearded Dragon's food?

It is common to supplement a dragon's diet with calcium, vitamin D3, and multivitamins, especially during growth. New research shows that if you feed and maintain your lizard's environment correctly, these supplements don't make that much difference. You must always have a veterinarian of your trust to accompany the

development of your animal so that he will indicate the best food management for your pet.

24. How long my Bearded Dragon can live without food?

Never, under any circumstances, leave your young Bearded Dragon without food. They have no reserves and will quickly perish.

Adult dragons can go without food for some weeks if it's too cold in their environment. However, under perfect keeping conditions, be sure to feed them for more than five days.

25. Why is my Bearded Dragon turning black?

Darkening happens for numerous reasons. Darkening the body can be a normal behavior when the dragon is basking or in the water, as well as when showing off to a female or opponents. Altering the color, especially in the beard, to black is also very common in situations of stress, fear, or conflict. They can also darken in low-light environments, thus increasing light absorption.

It can be either a common sign or a dark color that indicates something is wrong.

You should observe the color of the animal and the behavior it is exhibiting at the moment.

Only after crossing that information will you be able to know if the darkening is something normal or a symptom that something is wrong.

26. Why is my Bearded Dragon puffed up?

They can get puffed up for a few reasons.

It is common to see dragons doing this when they are in the basking spot and showing off. However, it is also normal for them to puff up in the bath water.

But beardies bloat their bodies to appear more prominent and frightening in stressful situations. In these cases, it is usually followed by behaviors such as opening the mouth, darkening the beard, head movements, and shaking the tail.

27. Why is my Bearded Dragon tail pointing up?

The straight tail, pointing upwards, is another sign where the Bearded

Dragon expresses itself. It could be a sign of alertness or excitement, or they could just be drying their tail after a shower. It's not a sign of concern; it's a behavior mostly seen when the animal is hunting or courting a female.

28. Why is my Bearded Dragon bobbing or waving its head?

Bobbing the head is a clear sign that the beardie is on alert or communicating that it is not very comfortable. It is also a sign of communication between them; waving their heads, they recognize each other.

Bearded Dragons use this strategy for the same reasons as when puffed up. To intimidate, to appear bigger, to try to attract the female's attention, etc., and to stay alert, observing a wider area around them.

29. Which are the Bearded Dragon's common diseases?

The Bearded Dragons' terrariums are usually the ideal place for the appearance of various pathogens.

If your lizard is healthy, it will hardly contract any disease, but if the reptile is weak from some lack of care, it will be easy to have some illness that threatens its life. In Pogona, we usually find the following conditions:

- Metabolic Bone Disease (MDB)

The MDB is a condition that affects many species of reptiles kept in captivity and is probably the most common disease in bearded dragons. It is caused by a lack of calcium and vitamin D, which is usually the result of a poor diet and inadequate lighting (lack of UVA and UVB rays). Consequently, the animal's metabolism demineralizes the bones, making them more fragile.

- Hepatic Lipidosis

The consumption of excess fats causes hepatic lipidosis. This condition happens due to a poorly balanced diet or overeating. Consequently, fatty acids accumulate in the liver due to this irregular diet, directly affecting the animal's metabolism and health.

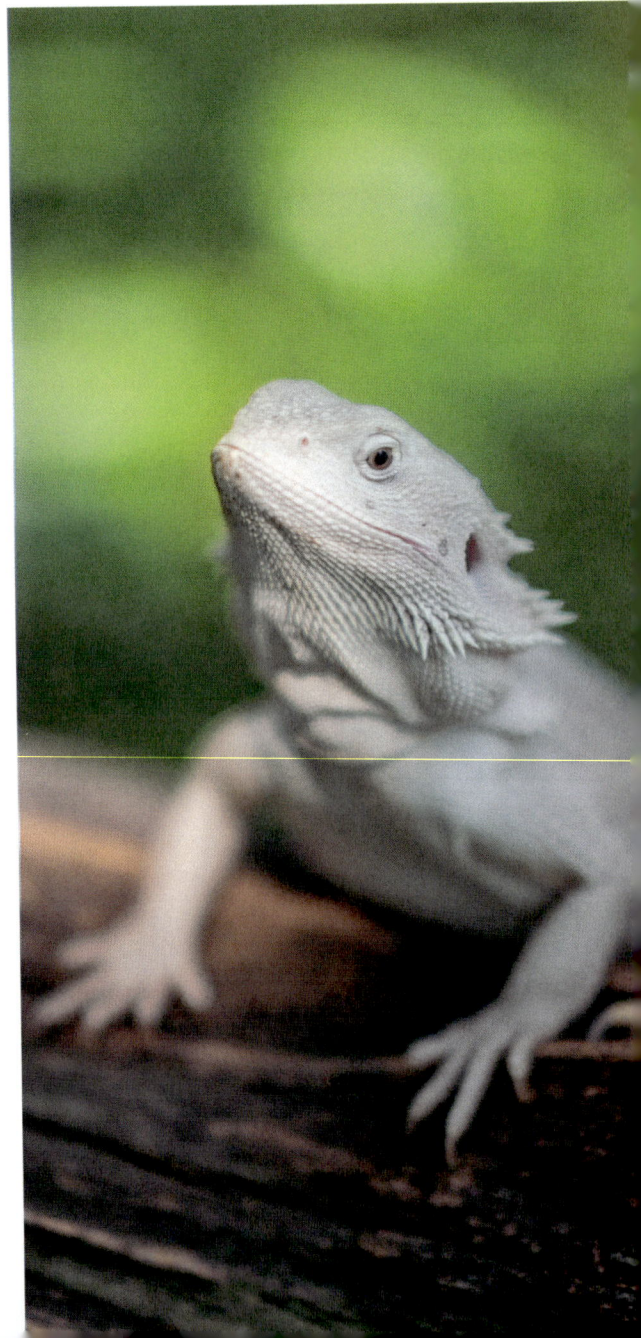

- **Hypovitaminosis (vitamin B1 deficiency)**
Thiamine, also known as vitamin B1, is a unique substance that is very important for the health of these animals, as it is necessary for the production of energy (acts directly in the metabolism of glucose, fatty acids, and amino acids), for the health of the nerves, muscles and mental function. In addition, it has antioxidant capabilities protecting cells from free radicals.

The deficiency of this vitamin is caused by irregular feeding, and some symptoms are animals becoming lethargic or having spasms. However, it is easily controlled through a balanced diet.

- **Disecdysis**
Dysecdysis refers to any problems that reptiles have during shedding. The low humidity of the environment usually causes these conditions, but some parasites and other diseases can also be involved. The most common symptoms are visual and easy to notice, with dry skin stuck or white spots on the dragon's body.

- **Stomatitis ('Mouth rot')**
Stomatitis is a common disease in reptiles and is characterized by infection of the oral mucosa and

adjacent tissues. During stomatitis, bacteria and fungi generally occur in the mouth and become pathogenic due to a drop in immunity.

- Ectoparasites

Skin parasites (ectoparasites) are frequently found among the common reptile parasites. Ectoparasites are common in farms and institutions that keep these animals.

- Yellow Fungus Disease

It is a type of dermatomycosis, that is, fungi that attack these animals' skin and are mainly seen in animals or under irregular keeping or stress.

- Virus infection (Adenovirus)

Adenoviruses are a group of viruses that cause various problems in reptiles and are easily transmissible.
Its main symptoms in captive animals are mainly associated with the animal's digestive tract, which alters the absorption of nutrients, generating undernourished animals or stunted growth.

- Intestinal infections (Pinworms and Coccidia)

A wide range of endoparasites (internal parasites) can occur in reptiles. In the case of the Bearded Dragon, among the main ones, we can mention coccidia and pinworms.

The infection is due to ingesting food (mainly vegetables) that have not been cleaned and disinfected or contacting other parasitized animals' feces.

30. Will my Bearded Dragon tail grow back?
Yes, broken tails will grow back.

The regeneration time depends on the animal's metabolism and even on the year's season – in summer, the new tail is born faster. The energy spent on tail regeneration comes at a high price: young individuals grow more slowly, and females in the reproductive phase produce fewer eggs.

All the tissues – vessels, muscles, nerves, etc. – are easily disconnected where the tail breaks. After that, the tail will regenerate,

but it will never be the same again. Instead, the new tail will be smaller, thicker, or crooked. The bone part also does not recover. In the part of the tail that regenerates, the vertebrae are replaced by a rod of cartilage.

31. What is Bearded Dragon's brumation?

Brumation is a state of lethargy, considered a dormancy type in which metabolism slows down. Some animals use it to cope with the drop in temperature in their habitat, similar to the hibernation process in mammals.

The bearded dragon is a reptile native to several deserts and semi-desert areas of Australia. This region experiences large thermal fluctuations, so, unsurprisingly, the species brumates during the wild's

coldest months of the year.

Even if you have a blanket of heat and light available, the bearded dragon will likely seek refuge in the coldest part of the terrarium during the winter. During this time, the animal will stop eating and be less active. Many bearded dragons do brumation for the first time in their second year of life, while others never do so.

Common Care Mistakes

1. About impulsive buys

The world of exotic animals is as fascinating as it is dangerous. Many reptiles and amphibians are kept as pets, but not all adapt well to life in captivity; some have toxins and poisons. To this is added the fact that some of these animals are taken from their natural environment to be sold, which is unethical and harmful to the environment.

Having a reptile at home is not just a responsibility for the specimen but the entire ecosystem. As dozens of surveys indicate, thousands of species of exotic animals are at risk of disappearing, partly due to the sale and removal of adult individuals from their natural environment. If you want to have a lizard at home, you should always check the origin of the animal.

Never buy or adopt an animal on impulse without thinking about and preparing everything the animal needs. For example, think that when you acquire a Bearded Dragon, it will be under your care for more than a decade, and you must have the social and financial conditions to keep them healthy all that time.

Acquiring any animal as a pet without evaluating the fundamental conditions to keep it leads to neglect and abandonment.

2. Tips for choosing your first Bearded Dragon

As previously mentioned, if you still need to gain experience with these animals, choose to purchase adult specimens. Dragon babies, as cute and cuddly as they are, require infinitely more work and care than adults. Always get animals from well-known breeders with a good reputation, ask to meet the parents, and observe to see if all animals are healthy if the sick are separated and how the breeder takes care of his animals.

3. Tips for housing and keeping your Bearded Dragon

Always maintain the ideal humidity and temperature for your dragons. Remember that they are animals from places like deserts and savannahs, so avoid elements of tropical terrariums like lakes and waterfalls. These can raise the humidity of the area. Make sure to keep the terrarium always sanitized and with good ventilation; this prevents the spreading diseases such as fungi and mites. Pogona can be kept in groups without problems, but in some cases, it may generate food competition. Therefore, we again emphasize the importance of being attentive during feeding. If this occurs, feed problematic individuals separately.

You can keep your bearded dragon along with other species, such as Blue Tongue Lizards. Make sure the species are environmentally compatible. Never keep your dragons with snakes or other predatory animals.

When feeding them, provide the amount of food the dragon will consume at that moment, and never leave food for later. Remember never to offer larvae and insects that are dead. Instead, offer them alive or right after you proceed with the proper slaughter.

As we have already seen, correct lighting is necessary for the animal to metabolize essential vitamins and minerals, so provide a basking area with direct sunlight or artificial light specifically for reptiles.

4. Controlling diseases, illnesses, and other conditions

The vast majority of diseases and illnesses in captive bearded dragons are caused by poor handling of the animal and its environment. Because of this, we consistently reinforce the importance of knowing and keeping an eye on your animals and having specialists' help.

In this regard, we have some considerations:

- **Habitat conditions:** Bearded Dragons depend on a controlled environment to keep their blood warm and a healthy metabolism. Therefore, any change can have severe consequences for your health. However, the parameters of temperature, humidity, and lighting are the ones that most impact the animal.

- **Diet:** Maintaining the diet of omnivorous animals requires a little more attention and work on the part of your owner, to achieve a healthy and perfectly balanced diet. This factor is crucial because an adequate diet keeps the body vigorous and allows it to face pathologies. In addition, a wide variety of nutritional problems can cost the reptile its life.

- **Hygiene:** Keeping your pet's environment clean and free of feces and leftover food is essential when keeping animals in

captivity. In this way, we mainly avoid the spread of disease and the low immunity of animals. Maintain an impeccable cleaning routine, and remember that reptiles can transmit diseases to you and other animals, so always sanitize your hands before and after cleaning their environment or holding them in your hand.

- **Accidents:** Any physical injury suffered by the reptile can lead to severe pathology, so treating it promptly and correctly is better.

In this book, we covered the most common questions to successfully keeping a unique Bearded Dragon and an incredible Bearded Dragon enclosure. Hopefully, you now have a better idea of what it is like to keep a Bearded Dragon as a pet. As you can see, Bearded Dragons are incredibly resistant lizards with exciting and curious behavior. If you like to keep lizards that interact with you and exhibit a Jurassic appearance, prepare your terrarium and go for these incredible Dragons!

Bearded Dragon Word Search

Find and circle the words.

A	S	D	F	G	H	J	I	K	L	O	P	M
U	K	B	H	G	L	I	Z	A	R	D	N	S
S	T	R	A	N	S	L	U	C	E	N	T	H
T	Z	U	Y	U	B	Q	A	F	T	U	Z	E
R	X	M	T	I	V	D	O	C	I	L	E	D
A	C	A	R	O	C	S	Z	G	Y	I	X	D
L	V	T	W	P	O	G	O	N	A	L	C	I
I	B	I	N	C	U	B	A	T	I	O	N	N
A	N	O	E	P	X	B	A	S	K	I	N	G
N	M	N	Q	A	Z	E	X	H	U	G	V	A

POGONA

AUSTRALIAN

BASKING

SHEDDING

BRUMATION

INCUBATION

TRANSLUCENT

DOCILE

LIZARD

Solution at Page 45

Download Five Bearded Dragon Posters

Scan w/your Camera to Download!

A Message From The Author

Hello from Oliver and her mom! We're the creators of The World of Rare Pets series of books.

Our hope is that you and your loved ones enjoy each and every book we create. It's our mission to reduce impulsive buying of rare pets & educate children beforehand so that they know what it's like to keep a pet responsibly.

We are no big publishing house with tons of money to throw in marketing efforts, so the only way to spread the word about our books is you, our lovely customers. If you like our book, please consider giving us your **honest feedback with a review on Amazon.** When you post a review on Amazon it really makes a huge difference towards helping a small business like ours.

We sincerely appreciate your purchase and for supporting our small business.

References

Brattstrom, B. H. (1971). Social and thermoregulatory behavior of the bearded dragon, Amphibolurus barbatus. Copeia, 484-497.

Cadena, V., Rankin, K., Smith, K. R., Endler, J. A., & Stuart-Fox, D. (2018). Temperature-induced colour change varies seasonally in bearded dragon lizards. Biological Journal of the Linnean Society, 123(2), 422-430.

Cannon, M. J. (2003, October). Husbandry and veterinary aspects of the bearded dragon (Pogona spp.) in Australia. In Seminars in Avian and Exotic Pet Medicine (Vol. 12, No. 4, pp. 205-214). WB Saunders.

Craig, M. D., Garkaklis, M. J., Hardy, G. E. S. J., Grigg, A. H., Grant, C. D., Fleming, P. A., & Hobbs, R. J. (2007). Ecology of the western bearded dragon (Pogona minor) in unmined forest and forest restored after bauxite mining in south-west Western Australia. Australian Journal of Zoology, 55(2), 107-116.

De Vosjoil, P., Sommella, T. M., Mailloux, R., Donoghue, S., & Klingenberg, R. J. (2016). The Bearded Dragon Manual: Expert Advice for Keeping and Caring for a Healthy Bearded Dragon. Fox Chapel Publishing.

Fan, M., Stuart-Fox, D., & Cadena, V. (2014). Cyclic colour change in the bearded dragon Pogona vitticeps under different photoperiods. PloS one, 9(10), e111504.

Jacobson, E. R., Kopit, W., Kennedy, F. A., & Funk, R. S. (1996). Coinfection of a bearded dragon, Pogona vitticeps, with adenovirus-and dependovirus-like viruses. Veterinary Pathology, 33(3), 343-346.

Julian, A. F., & Durham, P. J. K. (1982). Adenoviral hepatitis in a female bearded dragon (Amphibolurus barbafus). New Zealand veterinary journal, 30(5), 59-60.

Raiti, P. (2012). Husbandry, diseases, and veterinary care of the bearded dragon (Pogona vitticeps). Journal of Herpetological Medicine and Surgery, 22(3-4), 117-131.

Salomies, L., Eymann, J., Khan, I., & Di-Poï, N. (2019). The alternative regenerative strategy of bearded dragon unveils the key processes underlying vertebrate tooth renewal. Elife, 8, e47702.

Smith, K. R., Cadena, V., Endler, J. A., Porter, W. P., Kearney, M. R., & Stuart-Fox, D. (2016). Colour change on different body regions provides thermal and signalling advantages in bearded dragon lizards. Proceedings of the Royal Society B: Biological Sciences, 283(1832), 20160626.

Throckmorton, G. S., De Bavay, J., Chaffey, W., Merrotsy, B., Noske, S., & Noske, R. (1985). The mechanism of frill erection in the bearded dragon Amphibolurus barbatus with comments on the jacky lizard A. muricatus (Agamidae). Journal of morphology, 183(3), 285-292.

A	S	D	F	G	H	J	I	K	L	O	P	M
U	K	B	H	G	L	I	Z	A	R	D	N	S
S	T	R	A	N	S	L	U	C	E	N	T	H
T	Z	U	Y	U	B	Q	A	F	T	U	Z	E
R	X	M	T	I	V	D	O	C	I	L	E	D
A	C	A	R	O	C	S	Z	G	Y	I	X	D
L	V	T	W	P	O	G	O	N	A	L	C	I
I	B	I	N	C	U	B	A	T	I	O	N	N
A	N	O	E	P	X	B	A	S	K	I	N	G
N	M	N	Q	A	Z	E	X	H	U	G	V	A

POGONA   SHEDDING   TRANSLUCENT

AUSTRALIAN   BRUMATION   DOCILE

BASKING   INCUBATION   LIZARD

Made in the USA
Middletown, DE
29 May 2024

55010187R00027